You Don't Have the Right to Remain Silent

How to Turn Your Story into a Play

Khalia S. Parker Preyer

Copyright © 2021 by KP2 Writes, LLC

All rights reserved. This book or any portion thereof may not be reproduced or used in any manner whatsoever without the express written permission of the publisher except for the use of brief quotations in a book review.

Printed in the United States of America

First Printing, 2021

ISBN: 978-1-7350896-1-4
Edited & Formatted by Show Your Success
Published by KP2 Writes, LLC

Dedication

This is for every person that reads a play or walks into a theatre to see a play and says "I can do that." I believe you.

It's also to every person that sees disservice and wants to change it and knows theatre is the best way. I believe you.

I do not take it lightly that every one of you has a story to tell. So use this recipe to get it written: 1 dose of love, two scoops of the arts, and a heap of culturally relevant materials is the recipe to fix theworld.

Table of Contents

Foreword vii

Acknowledgment ix

Introduction xi

Chapter 1: Know Your Voice 1

Chapter 2: Start with a Theme 15

Chapter 3: Decide on a Structure 23

Chapter 4: Create Interesting Characters 35

Intermission 47

Chapter 5: Be the Dramaturg 53

Chapter 6: Find Your Target Audience 61

Chapter 7: Be the Architect of Your Play 71

Conclusion 79

Curtain Call 81

Red Carpet 83

Foreword

Being a part of the publishing world since 2014 has taught me so much. The main thing is that EVERYONE deserves to have their story told. However, I believe that it is a way to share your story so that it is attractive to everyone who sees and hears it. What Khalia has put together in this book, I believe, is genius! Turning your story into a play is something amazing. I think that anyone who wants to see their story come to life on a stage needs this book.

In this book, Khalia shares so many similar tips that I share when it comes to writing a "How-To" book, but she also adds some unique gems on how your story turned into a play can impact so many key people. If you know in your heart, people need to hear your story. An important step is to get it on stage. This book is going to help you with that. Not only will this book help you to learn how to get started, but she also offers coaching to take it even further. Be sure to take notes and get ready to be inspired. I promise you. She has me over here ready to put on a stage play!

Congratulations Khalia! This book is going to change so many lives! Hopefully, we will get tickets to your stage play about your life one day soon. And to the person reading this book, congratulations to you in advance.

~ Taurea Vision Avant
Queen of Book Profiting

Acknowledgment

- DeMarcus A. Preyer
- Lorraine Payne
- Douglas Payne
- Lyle and Janis Mosley
- Talmadge and Kenya Irvin
- Barbara Abel
- Sabrina Griffin
- Melvin Jackson
- Artisha Arthur
- Willa Kimble
- Camille Neely
- Letia Gale
- Yvonne King
- Juanita Porter
- Emma Graves
- Donna Jefferson
- Briana Gullet
- Sandra Allen Jones
- Ayanna Sallins
- Barbara Ann Williams
- Khamari Dimanche
- Portia L. Brantley
- Laura Williams
- Tyra McBeth Simon
- Gwen Russell Green
- TaTanisha Shumpert
- Gloria Moss
- G. L. Brown
- Jasmine Nicole Abel
- Cecille Bolton
- Denise Cook Godfrey
- Shirley Carter
- Johnny and Lucille Mosley

Acknowledgment

- Torrance and Christina Bryant
- Connie Freeman
- Patrick Broadus
- Amelia Morse Kolkmeyer
- Marc Allen, Sr.
- Rickey and Annika Culbreath
- Wess Walters
- Shereka Nottingham
- Deedria Faulker
- Sacha Hand
- Dwayne and Talya Parker
- Ashley Lott
- Leigh Ann Bain
- Alexcia Hollis Moore
- Samuel and Latoya Blackmon
- Evelyn Myers
- Elektra Thompson
- Latonya Anderson
- Celeste Phoenix
- Pamela Liggins
- Salisha George
- Lawanda Grant
- T'Mya Tomlinson
- Yvonne King
- Connie Freeman
- Chris Freeman
- David Downin
- J'Neen Evans
- Cassandra Collins

Introduction

Congratulations to you on this journey of telling your story. It is not by accident that you've received this book *You DON'T have the Right to Remain Silent: How to Turn Your Story into a Play.* It is not a coincidence that you have chosen the best coach to help you navigate the world of playwriting. I appreciate you entrusting me to help you go from page to stage, a challenge many authors neglect.

Many books offer lessons on writing a stage play, but none before this one stresses the fact that the play you create should be free of bias and stereotypes and that it should highlight and challenge issues in the society in which you dwell. Through this book for future playwrights, I want to address the misrepresentation in theatre and the compromising of artists to produce work that isn't culturally rewarding. With over 15 years of theatre and theatre education experience. I salute the work of playwrights before me. Yet, this coach is on a mission. I want to help you turn your

Introduction

story into a play in a culturally appropriate way, a journey I have grown to love.

I know what you are probably thinking: There are already so many plays. With a plethora of theatre experience, however, I know that many generations are being left out of reading and producing plays that reach certain ages, races, andinterests. In this book, I will provide you with methods and tips and help you identify your target audience. I plan to help you get a sold-out show full of rewarding themes and valuable feedback.

Not only do I want you to embrace your story, but I also want you to understand that someone's destiny is tied to your purpose. Failure to share your story can be detrimental to your audience. Withholding your story is playwright homicide. Unlike when you're given the Miranda Rights, we do not have the right to remain silent about issues plaguing our community.

Maybe you don't know where to start. Maybe you are stuck in the middle of something great and just need a little push from me to finish. Well, technically, I don't give little pushes; my passion makes me do too much at times. When I stumble across a play that I know will have a great impact on society, I just can't let go.

Introduction

I've been where you are plenty of times. I was somewhere between a genius idea and a post-production meeting, and I needed inspiration. I needed the motivation to finish, and I was fresh out of excuses. I put the pencil to my journal, and I wrote for an hour every day. When I forgot to write, I went back. I knew that if I continued to write my interesting stories, I would never have writer's block. The only wood I had to knock on was the one connected to the lead of my pencil.

Have you ever been invited to a stage to be honored for your work? My first stage was in front of many of my peers and adults. I was in 10th grade when my first play was honored by The National Association for the Advancement of Colored People (NAACP) through their program called The Afro-Academic, Cultural, Technological and Scientific Olympics (ACT-SO). That experience brought about my very first gold medal, my first flight, and my first testimony of how my writer's voice could change the world. I was among celebrities and simultaneously realized that my partnership was sealed with this civil rights organization that I would grow to love while doing what I love.

Introduction

I'm giving you a little bit of everything I learned along my journey as a playwright. I won't give you it all because I need you to buy my next book. I want you to read it all the way through the first time, read each chapter in the order of your choice the second time, and then read it again and make highlights. What? I am preparing you for your readers. When you write your play, I encourage you to imagine the director reading your work three times: once all the way through, then reading the scenes individually, and finally going back, notating, and highlighting. Put it in the atmosphere, and it will happen.

Stop worrying, stop waiting, start reading *You Don't Have the Right to Remain Silent: How to Turn Your Story into a Play.* Make a difference in this society with your culturally relevant play. Provide jobs for theatre professionals and theatre lovers. Save somebody's life.

Culturally Relevant,
Khalia S. Parker Preyer

CHAPTER 1

Know Your Voice

John 10:27: My sheep listen to my voice, I know them, and they follow me (NIV).

We're not Jesus, but we can relate to wanting people to listen to us and follow us. To get your audience prepared to see your work, they have to recognize your voice. As they learn to recognize your voice, getting them to listen will be simple. In this chapter, you will learn how to identify your voice as a mechanism for change through journaling. You will also know that your voice is unique and why writing your story helps you avoid negative or dishonest stereotypes in theatre. No one will follow you if they are unsure about your message and how they can apply it to their lives.

Focus on Self

I began by writing in my journal every day. Your journal is a surrogate that will help to nurture you and guide you until you meet the ears you seek. As a teenager, I recorded in my journal all evidence that was later used against me. I went to the skating rink this one time and left my journal sitting on my aunt's couch. By the conclusion of the day, she knew more about me than I knew about myself. Years later, I returned to that journal while searching for content for my play. I learned so much about myself by reading my journal. Furthermore, I was introduced to characters that I wanted to write more about. These characters make great plays.

To find your voice, you have to do a lot of praying and meditating. You have to document life's journey and focus on SELF.

- **S-Stop judging yourself and others.** We all have pains and trauma that we don't want others to know about. We all have our deepest fears. Give yourself and others wiggle room to make and correct mistakes. No one on this earth is perfect. We strive to be like Christ and not to be Christ. There are different strokes for different folks. Practice your breathing, go swimming, and do yoga.

- **E-Evaluate your circles and corners**. Be mindful of the people and things you surround yourself with. If it's not working toward the plot you have envisioned for your life and God's plan for your life, it's okay to disconnect. We all get disappointed when the "call failed" statement goes across our phone screens, and we get the choice of letting it go or calling back again. Just like our phone screens, we get warning of when that relationship or friendship has failed. Stop reconnecting with bad connections. Just because your circle is thick doesn't mean that they are in your corner. Frequently remind yourself to take deep breaths. Be okay with going with the flow at times. Have your own back.

- **L-Live vibrantly and intentionally.** Pray, meditate, eat well, and get sleep. Don't forget to create and sustain your morning rituals. I reviewed my To-Do list the night before, so I already know what I have to look forward to. As a mother of toddlers, I realize it doesn't always go as planned, but as long as I remain positive and embrace the fact that it's God's plan, my days, weeks, months are productive, vibrant, and intentional. I recommend that you go to brunch if you want to be inspired and want to show yourself some gratitude. If brunch is not long enough, then take a vacation. You'll thank me later.

- **F-Fight for what you believe in.** We are living in dark times, many people will say, but when were the bright times? My Aunt Rosemary's favorite quote was, "Live for TODAY and take nothing for granted." I don't take for granted any opportunity to speak up for what I believe in, whether it be love, family, social justice, the arts, and/or women's health. Fredrick Douglass said, "If you don't stand for something, you'll fall for anything." I am standing, not falling for things I strongly believe in, like civil rights and support for children of inmates.

Be selfish so you can be selfless; that's the key! Before you read any part of this book, you have to agree to focus on your personal needs and be selfless in your community. Focus on self, and you will identify your voice. As I write about teenagers and try to understand things that teenagers go through, I often refer to the journals I have stored in my footlocker from my own High School experience.

Use the Arts

"Before a child talks they sing. Before they write they draw. As soon as they stand they dance. Art is fundamental to human expression."
- Phylicia Rashad

Theatre is life! It's a life full of laughter and tears, joy, and the ability to face all fears. In middle school, my math teacher would say, "Everybody has free drama." I know she was probably referring to my gift of creativity, the passion in my voice, and my ability to tell great stories, but it took me a few years to figure out that the drama was free. Not only is it free, but I've lived to find out theatre is for everyone. Theatre is a language, full of jargon and various dialects, and that's perfectly fine. Its diversity is beautiful, and once you understand that the show must go on, you get it.

A mirror of life, theatre allows us to see things how we expect them and how we would never expect them. Theatre advocates for things we are passionate about. Theatre drives our imagination wild as it provides a creative home for all of us. That's why I love theatre. It's the essence of our being formulated into many characters and settings.

You can be yourself and anyone else while maintaining open perspectives. There is a place for you in the arts, in theatre, in the theater, on stage, backstage, and in the audience. Theatre teaches us what and how to appreciate. We get so caught in frivolous things in this world that we forget to appreciate the moments that matter. Yes, all arts teach a message, but theatre delivers the message in an intimate way from opening night to curtain call, and then we go on and make changes. That's why I love the arts.

Make it Culturally Relevant (Avoid Stereotypes)

Representation matters. As theatre is a mirror of life and a mechanism to tell human stories, we are tasked with investigating human experiences. Yes, theatre involves taking risks. We take risks with our acting, staging, and designs, but we should not take risks with incorrect stereotypes, as those risks can be detrimental to your story.

Sadly, if one is not careful, stereotypes become an identity.

While theatre is responsible for representing human identity, we want to ensure that inappropriate stereotypes becoming identity are avoided. Try your best!

The characters we write represent the identity of another human being. Everyone (knowing and unknowing) wants to see themselves on stage.

If you can fathom how important it is for people to see themselves on stage, then you'd understand these two things I've learned about humans and theatre: Everyone wants to be noticed, and no one wants to feel like they are by themselves. Everyone wants to matter, whether it's their look or their feelings.

It's funny that I equate identity in theatre to Hamlet's famous line written by William Shakespeare: "to be, or not to be". Everyone wants to BE.

Can you recall the feeling of viewing an artistic work and walking out of the theater with not one character that you can identify with? It is the theatre's responsibility to make sure everyone's story is told. As a culturally relevant specialist, I want to ensure all work under my umbrella is culturally appropriate. I want the work to be aligned with WEB Dubois's "For Us, By Us" notion.

How do we align with that? We write our own stuff. Yes . . . You.

Our audience wants characters on stage that look, feel, and speak like them. They want characters that they can identify with. That's what keeps theatre in business. That's what keeps people reading our plays. We want to be legitimized, so we don't feel ostracized in the world of theatre. Underrepresentation is a direct correlation to the oppression in our society. You, as a writer, have to understand that. Only recently has the diversity of our communities begun to genuinely be represented in theatre. Plays with people of color as the leads working hard to achieve goals, with women of color being leaders and not servants, with children with disabilities as leads. I can go on and on.

Before you begin writing the script, I want you to examine clichés and stereotypes that we've subconsciously worked into our collective identity. I forgive you in advance. With who/what do you identify with?

That's super important in your "culturally relevant" journey as a writer.

Your Voice is Your Opinion and Should Be Incorporated into Your Work.

Secretly your audience sees your story unfolding through one set of eyes. And that's yours, the playwright. If there was ever a question of whether your voice matters, the answer is: it does now because it's your play. It's a matter of opinion. In families and friendships, we're taught that our opinion can get us in trouble. I always beg to differ with that teaching, and I am sure that is what got me slapped in the mouth a few times at the dinner table. For instance, "Why are we praying for sister Susan, and you don't even like her? Shouldn't we be praying for that Walkman I asked for Christmas? The one I can record the latest hits on and play it back?"

Now is your time, Playwright, to incorporate your opinion into your script, even the smallest of such. Your expertise is not the same as any other playwrights. Don't act on anyone else's opinion; use yours instead. You can do that by playing a game of Unpopular Opinion. I'll demonstrate:

Unpopular Opinion #1: I disagree with the statement that cats are the cleanest pets.

To me, house dogs are the cleanest pets. I have no problem throwing them in the tub with some great smelling pet shampoo every other day. Many will argue that you should only wash your pet bi-weekly and groom them monthly. The truth is I don't even have a dog currently, but I have an opinion, and I can work my opinion into my play.

Unpopular Opinion #2: Not making social plans until the last minute works for me. I don't like to make promises on other people's time. And honestly, I don't know how I'm going to feel on the day or time of your event.

To keep unity and smoothness in my friendships and other relationships, I had decided to be more upfront ahead of time. The same goes for your script; knowing your opinion makes a script that is unified and smooth to your audience.

My little opinion is just an appetizer; imagine incorporating other, more intimate opinions into your work.

Unpopular Opinion #3: I don't stay silent about family issues and family secrets that hurt other family members physically and mentally. That may be your cue to slap me in the mouth, but not speaking up about things can destroy a loved one and can hurt people. Although people may not want to read a book about it, if they are in a theater watching characters on the stage looking for the one they can relate to, they may recognize the character with an opinion like mine. I can offer advice in my script that can push them to a breakthrough. Your Voice is a matter of intimacy, and you should consider sharing it with the world. Good writers allow themselves to see and explore other people's opinions to gain insight into how other characters may feel in the play.

Now it's your turn. Take out your journal and play Unpopular Opinion. Write down your opinions on issues affecting you. It can be small opinions that give insight, an opinion that provides unity and smoothness in relationships, or an intimate opinion. I also encourage you to join in. Your very next opinion could be the theme of your next stage play. Go to: bonus.bookedplaywright.com.

Notes

Notes

CHAPTER 2

Start with a Theme

———

"The greatest gift is not being afraid to question."
— Ruby Dee

Start with a Theme

Many playwrights and theater philosophers have their say on what they think is the most important attribute to a play. I was always taught to start with the plot. For me, it didn't quite work. Somewhere along with my experience in theater, I learned that the thing is the most important aspect of the play. In the meat of any conflict, my first question is, what's the issue? I know that if I could get to the issue, then I can try to get others to see things my way. Every now and then, between shows, I have the opportunity to watch a little TV and a little bit of news. I often stumble across issues that are important to me, like educational law, public health, social injustice, and politics. Have you ever had an issue that hit hard and was so near and dear to your heart that you couldn't wait to tell someone what you thought about it? Have you ever had an issue that you told someone about and they just couldn't relate to? Starting with the theme creates great content, and I highly recommend using this strategy to make culturally relevant content.

Start with a Theme

Identify Your Burning Question After Considering Universal Themes

No matter your geographical location or what culture you identify with, we all have themes that we can connect to. These themes, for my English scholars, are called universal themes. Universal themes include but are not limited to: beating the odds, fear of failure, the quest for knowledge, safety, seizing the moment, parent- child relationships, religion, and pride. Have you ever been in class and had a question that you just couldn't wait to ask, so your raised hand began to shake, and your foot subconsciously began to tap? That's the feeling of having a burning question. A question that was so good that it hurt to keep it inside. Here is a burning question that I always like answered: why do you run into your ex when you look and feel like you're having an allergic reaction to life? Consider how many movies and plays begin on that topic? We all want to look and feel good at all times, but in front of our ex, we want to be able to say we've never felt or looked better.

Will you allow me to use a burning question about love to assess whether you understand where I'm going? Tell me about a moment you came of age or became an adult. Oh, it's too soon? You weren't ready for that question? That question can be answered in many ways. It doesn't have to be sexual at all. It could be a happy story or a significantly traumatizing story. Everyone has various stories about love. You sharing your story can help some embrace the love they have been receiving or reject a love that's unhealthy.

Assess How You Want Your Character to Grow

Theatre production is community service. Local theaters work extremely hard to provide a platform where people can express themselves free of judgment. As a playwright, you want your work to get into communities around the world. Your goal is to serve someone with your play, right? The characters you create are the cooks, and your future actors are the servers that will ultimately deliver your satisfying script. No one wants to stay stagnant or leave the theater in the same mindset that they came in. As a playwright,

Start with a Theme

your passion helps other people make choices toward their destiny. Even if they cannot figure out their destiny before leaving the theater, they want their next move to be their best move.

Each and every time you write a play, you should decide how you want your audience member to exit, even if you only reach one. You must also note that you are speaking into their lives through actors. What line do you want them to remember? What characteristics should they bring home with them? Pre-determine the takeaways for your audience, and you will be on your way to a successful script. Write the play, secure your royalties, and serve your audience. Many producers pay top dollar for the perfect message on programs and topics important to them. The bonus is you'll also be fulfilling your purpose.

Push Past the Cliché

Powerful themes are not basic clichés. No one wants to see your play and learn, "What goes around comes around," or "We learned that in grade school." You don't want your audience to think that you can't develop original thought or

Start with a Theme

that you are too lazy to do it. Push beyond the tired, uninspiring themes. Also, don't tell the audience what they must do because you will find that they are just as stubborn as you, the playwright. State your opinion with the takeaway in mind. Allow them to explore the scenario, make deductions, and obtain their own ideas. If you provide them with alternative opinions via other characters, they will get your message.

You will find that clichés can be a communication barrier to certain cultures, for they can be specific to a language and/or a location. "Get home before the street likes to come on" my mom used to tell me all the time. Now, I live in Georgia. You will not find many if any street lights. So when addressing my children, I now have to push past my mother's cliché and tell them what time I am requesting their presence. I may also have to tell them what is designated and where to find it. Similarly, I encourage my clients to push beyond cliché and incorporate a direct message. Just like in football everyone wants a quarterback that can get the ball to the right receiver without getting intercepted. Playwright, you are the quarterback of your script.

Start with a Theme

Notes

Start with a Theme

Notes

CHAPTER 3

Decide on a Structure

"The most common way people give up their power is by thinking they don't have any."
— *Alice Walker*

Decide on a Structure

Many would argue that theater began in ancient Greece in about 500 BC. I say Theatre derived in Africa, somewhere in or near West Africa to be exact. In college, I learned about Griots and the Griot traditions. Many of the Griot traditions are still alive today. Griots are storytellers. Griot's used their storytelling skills to give guidance, provide knowledge, and offer praise.

My ancestors are my favorite Griots. To this day, if I want to hear a story full of wisdom and a little bit of exaggeration, I will sit on the porch with my grandparents. What is the secret to creating great stories? Maybe it's the pacing, or maybe it's the choreography, or maybe it's the music they incorporate into their folktales as my heart beats like a drum. I remember my grandfather telling me the story about his older brother, who was in a war. I don't quite remember which war, but I know he was on the ground shooting the buttons off of another army man's shirt. Was it the truth? Maybe some of it was. Was it full of exaggeration? I bet you my house that most of it was.

As a playwright, you're going to have to acknowledge what makes great stories. You will also have to analyze the structure of those stories to create good work. Feel free to read good and bad plays to develop good storytelling skills and structure.

Meet My Friend Aristotle

The great Greek philosopher, scientist, and poet Aristotle contributed much to the theatre. He tutored Alexander the Great, so you know he was a big deal. He maintained that theatre was not only meant to enlighten but also to entertain and that theatre derived from one's desire to imitate. Aristotle gave us the blueprint of a good play.

He introduced the plot as the most essential element in playwriting. If you are following along and read the previous chapter, you will find that I did not say the plot wasn't important. What I did say was that I started with the theme. Again that's my method and my philosophy. Aristotle says that you need six elements to make a play good. Every playwright has their own method and their own philosophers that they follow. I like to stick with Aristotle. Much of his work references tragedies, but I enjoy applying his principles to all of my dramas.

According to the greatest Greek philosopher, you must have the following recipe for a good play:

Plot - Beginning, Middle, End (storyline)

Characters - Static or Dynamic individual(s) working toward a goal

Theme: The thought the playwright was trying to communicate. The idea you want the audience to leave with.

Diction or Dialogue - How the people in the world of the play communicate.

Music - Sounds to set the mood and enhance the play.

Spectacle: A nice set or visuals to communicate the location.

Each element plays a major role in the audience's experience, and altogether they make a good play. The Greek playwright Sophocles' play *Oedipus Rex* is the most used play to highlight elements of a good play. If you haven't read the Oedipus trilogy, you are truly missing a treat.

Dramatic Structure/Freytag's Pyramid

Aristotle emphasized the plot structure to notate the beginning, middle, and end of a play.

Decide on a Structure

Gustav Freytag was a German playwright and novelist who created a pyramid that helps us identify important parts (five) of the plot and shows dramatic structure. Many great writers use this structure today.

EXPOSITION - The exposition provides the introduction. It is where we identify the given circumstance of the story. The who, what, when, and where is identified in the exposition. Who's your protagonist? Antagonist?

*INCITING INCIDENT - The inciting incident is typically placed between the exposition and the rising action. When you want to start a fire, you light a match, right? It's the same with your story. You have to encourage or stir up drama or conflict.

RISING ACTION - Uh oh, what action did your protagonist take? In the words of Michael Jackson, "if you want to be starting something. You got to be starting SOMETHING".

CLIMAX - The highest point of action is the climax. It is the peak. You know that awkward moment you are on a roller coaster, and you get to the very top, and you can see the whole city? I have a love/hate relationship with that feeling. I recently went to Carowinds and hopped on the Fury 325. I was nervous going up, but when I saw where the "Carolina's intersect" 325-ft in the air, I thought I would lose it. I knew that there was no way to go back, you can only go forward, and all I could do was hold my breath, close my eyes, and DROP. The climax gives the protagonist an ultimatum. You must make a decision.

FALLING ACTION - This brings us to the falling action. What decision will your protagonist make? Will it change your protagonist for the better? The worst? I'm not a fan of commercials when watching my favorite movies, plays, and television shows, but I detest the commercial after the falling action. We are rooting for our protagonist! Will he or she win?

RESOLUTION - Be it resolved that the resolution is final. What was the solution to the problem presented between the exposition and rising action? How will we go on?

Acts and Scenes

As you continue to focus on the structure of your play, it is important that you know that the acts and scenes are vital to sequencing and separating the narration of the story. If it's not a one-act play, your good play has to be broken up into at least two major parts. Okay, three if you think you're Tennessee Williams and five if you think you're William Shakespeare. Those major parts are called acts, and the subdivision of those acts are called scenes.

The struggle becomes real when people don't know the difference between an act and the scene. The primary indicator of a scene versus an act is its length and depth. A scene is a segment of an act. An act has progression, while a scene changes the tempo, the characters, even when it doesn't necessarily change location. Acts can be 30 to about 60 minutes long, while a scene is much shorter. I break most of my plays up this way: exposition-> rising action -> climax -> end of act one-> falling action ->resolution-> end of act two. Think of the scenes as a platform for negotiations. Sometimes both parties in the scene will get what they want. Sometimes one party will prevail over the other obstacle or person. Sometimes neither party will get what they want and the negotiations will have to be worked out later in the play. Just add more tactics and keep on moving. Don't get stuck.

Fire the Narrator

In any fiction work, the narrator is the person responsible for providing an account of the events in your story. They determine the point of view of the play. I recommend that you fire the third-party narrator in your play and allow your protagonist to work their magic. No one wants to come to your play and see a person telling them about the action ahead. When I open a play and see the role of NARRATOR, I immediately say to myself, "What a waste of time." I want you to show me and not tell me what's going on in a scene. Why wouldn't you add the events of your story inside of the dialogue?

Your audience may not be from Missouri, but we all have attributes of being from the "show me" state. I recommend writing a witness, a waitress, an angel, sharing clues about where they are and what they have experienced. They could tell what

Decide on a Structure

they know about the protagonist's perspective or even be a know-it-all type of character and tell everybody's perspective. Whatever you decide, I do not want a person standing on a stage, possibly behind a podium, with a microphone, telling the audience what to look forward to in the next scene. Provide great details in your work through the actors, so they'll have to use their bodies, their facial expressions, and their voice to communicate their perspectives. Don't bore your audience. Incorporate the narration into your characters, and your audience may stick around after intermission.

Notes

Notes

Notes

CHAPTER 4
Create Interesting Characters

"Perhaps the mission of an artist is to interpret beauty to people - the beauty within themselves."
- Langston Hughes

Create Interesting Characters

God was extremely creative when He created people. He added hips and curves, made our lips plump, allowed our eyes to gaze, and He didn't stop with just physical attributes. He gave us hobbies and personalities. Some of us have bigger personalities, and some just a little. Yet, none of us are exactly the same, and that's what makes us beautiful and unique.

As you continue to write your play, allow yourself to create and build multi-dimensional characters. I encourage you to put a lot of thought into the characters that you create. Humans are not perfect so neither should your character be. Characters should have obstacles and flaws just like us. Look at characters from famous TV shows and movies. One of my favorite characters is from a 1990's sitcom, *Clueless*. Cher and Dionne weren't just best friends. They were in high school, wore interesting attire, and shared an inspirational and interracial friendship. While Cher is filthy rich and has everything a girl could want, she still has some challenges. Good playwrights make their characters unique but not outlandish. You must equip your characters to live in the world that you create.

Identify the Protagonist

There are two types of characters that we use when writing a play. **Static** means that at the end of the play, the character remained the same. **Dynamic** means the character changes throughout the play. I'm not really a fan of static characters. I like to write characters that go through some struggles that shape them into who they really are. In chapter 3, I introduced you to my friend Aristotle. But I forgot to tell you about one other thing that Aristotle introduced. He said that somewhere in the plot your dramatic characters should go through a catharsis. Catharsis is a purge of emotions from pity to fear. It is not limited to the character; as your audience watches, they should also experience a catharsis.

Throughout most dramas, the audience subconsciously goes through many different emotions because they always pick the character they believe in. The audience tends to root for or against the main character. They may, in fact, root for the main character's adversary, the antagonist. Here's how we get our protagonist and antagonist. Most times, we are for the protagonist, hence the suffix.

Create Interesting Characters

Pro means good/for
Anti means against

When thinking of characters, you have to find out what they are for and what they are against. Sometimes it isn't the same, and such is life. To be honest, I am pro-life, but that doesn't mean I'm against women making the best decision for their bodies. Let me hop off of that before you all stop reading. We can talk about that later in the book. To understand people and to understand life and/or the world of plays is to know that sometimes it's:

Man vs. Self
Man vs. Man
Man vs. World

Make Your Characters the G.O.T.E. of Your Story.

I want to speak on a concept introduced to me in college by Robert Cohen. It is the G.O.T.E. method. He introduces G.O.T.E. as a way for actors to analyze characters in a script and based on my prior knowledge of theatre, I've learned to also use his strategy to write my plays. Your readers can analyze characters by their:

Goal

People take the characters we create in a text and start to believe in them. As readers, we desire to see multi-dimensional characters with goals just like us. What are some goals you have for your week? Your life? Maybe you want to catch a great movie this week. Maybe you want to publish five plays in your lifetime. Whatever goals you have, you should set both short-term and long- term goals. You should not just set one of each, either. A goal is what you want, right? I always want to go to the beach. Like us, we want your character to want something.

Obstacles

I told you that one of my goals is always to go to the beach, but there are obstacles to every goal. Work is an obstacle for me at the moment, though I'm blessed to have employment. I can't focus on writing while I'm on the beach because, more than likely, I'm not alone. The rain presents obstacles at times, too. What makes a story great is the obstacles. The best story has a main character with an obstacle. I like to call the biggest obstacle a character has a flaw. I'm ready to go to the beach on any day and at any time. My obstacle, however, is procrastination. Surely, I can drive 300+ miles to the beach today, but I won't because I've procrastinated with my script and will need to pack. Why am I not packed? You guessed it . . . my lack of planning highlights my gift of procrastination. What obstacles can your character have? Who can stop them from achieving their goal? The deeper, the better. We love drama! We want to see that thorn in their side unravel naturally.

Tactic

How will your character get to their goal? Will they lie, cheat, steal? Or will they plan, work, and balance? How a person gets what they want says a lot about their character. Many people like action movies and characters that choose violence. We, as playwrights, do not put violence on stage. We write the text with stage directions, and the director later interprets it. The actor interprets what their director provides them and becomes the character. The audience gains knowledge based on all of these interpretations. So, how will your character get what they want? What will they do? Do not hold back when creating these characters. Do not hesitate to go beyond the surface to create them.

The goal is to provide an exciting and engaging script no matter the content or style. Playwrights do not write violence. We write about events both historical and current, and we insert them into our work. If what we write is interpreted as explicit by our critics, then it's not on us as playwright. Theatre is a mirror of what's going on in our society. If someone finds it uncomfortable then the community needs to change. It's the audience's prerogative to interpret the play how they feel based on the character's goals, obstacles, and tactics. So, if you think a play is explicit, fascinating, imaginative, or gripping, don't just blame it on the playwright. It's mostly in your mind.

Expectation

You may have expected something more dramatic when you saw a play. You may have even expected something with lots of action or romance. Congratulations, you are human. Playwrights create characters based on their perception of human experiences. Helping or not helping a character reach their expectation makes the play either fulfilling or boring to the audience. The movie *Pursuit of Happiness* was long for me. The main character, Chris Gardner, played by Will Smith, was working hard to win. He was single, homeless, unemployed, and had many more problems. Yet, we wanted him to get a fulfilling job so he could make a living for himself and his son. Now, if your idea was for Christopher to meet a woman and live happily ever after by the end of the movie, you probably would have been disappointed. This movie may not have met your expectations. It was not a love story.

Your protagonist may or may not be the Greatest of All Times, but I expect you to build them on the four elements presented by Robert Cohen: Goals, Obstacles, Tactics, Expectations. If you use this technique to build your character, you'll be the Greatest of all times, G.O.A.T, at writing the next great play.

The Versus Battle

To understand people and to understand life and/or the world of plays is to know that sometimes it's:

>Man vs. Self
>Man vs. Man
>Man vs. World

I believe Marvel does such a good job with creating characters because sometimes their characters incorporate all three. Look at my man, the strong, green, Incredible Hulk, also known as Dr. Banner. The guy has some serious issues, and yes, he's labeled a monster based on how he was created in a lab using gamma rays. Watching the movie and reading about him tells us he has frog tendencies, and he's a little depressed. This world has been tough on Dr. Banner. In a few movies he is challenged by his mental illness and works hard to channel his anger. He may be indirectly responsible for the tree frog experiment that was originally performed on a frog taking its toll on him.

There you have it. Man vs. Self and Man vs. World, but I am sure you can find a whole lot of Man vs. Man in the movie there as well. Who is his rival? Dr. Banner works hard in a lab with many people and often snaps on them and destroys the place. He also fights villains like Juggernaut and even his ally Wolverine. As much as we love Dr. Banner's passionate side, many characters and antagonists have to reckon with Mr. Hulk, and, spoiler alert, they are not all bad guys. Any obstacle working against the goals of the protagonist in a story is labeled the antagonist. We don't necessarily have to agree with the writer's perspective, but it is still recognizable.

Write About People You Know.

I enjoy fellowshipping with people as I get to know them. Every now and then, I head to brunch or the mall and people watch. Pump the brakes. I'm not a stalker, yet I think I enjoy it so much because I can watch people. Yes, people-watching is a sport and a ritual. The mall is great, but you only get to indirectly interact with people. Maybe you have a rushed conversation with the cashier or the annoying employee that keeps asking if you need a dressing room or an awkward elevator conversation on the way to the next floor. I'm not a fan of trying on clothes in the store. I'd rather make the trip back to return the clothes. My little introverted self, I prefer authentic conversations with friends or acquaintances. That's where I get to learn so much about them. As playwrights, we work to build relationships with the characters we create. You have to spend time creating and building the characters we will write about. I encourage you to initiate this relationship with each of your characters before you find out their fate and/or destination.

It's important to develop multifaceted characters. Pay attention to their speech, opinions, effects on others, actions, and looks. You can create characters and allow the audience to infer who they truly are. You don't have to state the obvious when you're creating the characters. Your characters are not oblivious to the world they live in, and neither is your audience. They are pretty smart and can infer what is affecting the characters and predict what happens next. Remember, we show and not tell.

Exaggerate the Characters and Their Decisions.

All right, sometimes our friends and family are a little boring. Sticking with the same routine from day to day causes them to be as stagnant as some static characters. I encourage you to write about people you know but don't just stop there. You should add personalities and traits to make them multi-dimensional characters. You have to think of it as dating. No one wants just physical appearance. You enjoy their company based on how they act and the ways they interact with others. I want you to write about people you know, yes, but I also want you to exaggerate a little bit. Exaggerating characters will keep the people you're writing about discreet. Change their names, and they'll never know you are writing about them. Make your characters multifaceted.

Playwright Intermission

Tell us about a story from your childhood that explains who you are as a writer.

I didn't speak much in school. I was shy and picked on. I'd write stories and make friends to keep me company. My imaginary boyfriend was so real, I convinced my Mom he really existed. His name was Pete Hall.

Beverly Banks, Playwright
Owner of True Love Productions Studio
College Park, Georgia
FB: trueloveproductions
Instagram: trueloveproductions

Tell us about a story from your childhood that explains who you are as a writer.

"As a child, I watched The Never ending Story (Warner Bros). I used to listen to and change the lyrics to the theme song and make it my own. I wanted to use their melody and put my own words to it so that's the first things that I started actually writing: poetry and songs. And so that shows what type of writer I am.

I write creative nonfiction.

Sharell D. Luckett, Playwright
CEO of the Black Acting Methods Studio
Atlanta, Georgia
Website: www.blackactingmehods.com
FB:blackactingmethods
Instagram: blackactingmethods

What's the first hook that gets a new play started for you?

I usually start with a theme. It is usually something I want to address then I start writing. Then it's the characters. For instance, when I wrote my first play, it was an adaptation of Cinderella. I wanted my Cinderella to be black. When I co-wrote Luminosity, I wanted it to reflect the parables of black people in the industry. I am usually addressing a theme first.

Sharell D. Luckett, Playwright
CEO of the Black Acting Methods Studio
Atlanta, Georgia
Website: www.blackactingmehods.com
FB:blackactingmethods
Instagram: blackactingmethods

Create Interesting Characters

Most writers write a great deal about themselves. What have you, as a writer, learned about yourself? What wisdom have you gained from writing?

One of the most impactful times of my life or very critical part of my life was from 19 until about mid-'30s. I got married when I was 19. Writing for me was therapeutic because I didn't have any outlets, like other human beings that I could talk to who could really help me. For me, writing was like the sky's the limit. I have no limitations. I can write about what I want to. I don't care who gets offended.

Tiwanna M. Duncan, Playwright
Hartford, Connecticut

As a playwright with a voice, what steps do you think African Americans should be taking to correct some inequalities that our society presents?

Playwrights have a perfect forum to shout out injustices because when someone comes to see a play, they are seated in a dark room as the story unfolds before them. They are in a safe, no-judgment zone. In the dark, as the issues are portrayed in the light of the stage, the participant can deal with themselves as they watch. They can watch passively and pretend that the strong message didn't affect them personally, but a well-formed production jam-packed with issues will make the participant take notice, no matter if they want to or not. One thing is for sure; you can't un-hear what you heard or un-see what you saw.

Beverly Banks, Playwright
Owner of True Love Productions
College Park, Georgia
FB: trueloveproductions
Instagram: trueloveproductions

Notes

Notes

CHAPTER 5

Be the Dramaturg

"Everything influences playwrights. A playwright who isn't influenced is never of any use."
-Arthur Miller

As a playwright, our job is pretty demanding. We are inspired by our life experiencesand knowledge to create a work of art.

I recommend that you add another role to your job description. The role is a dramaturg, the person responsible for providing the director and ultimately the cast and crew vital information about the world of the play. As the playwright and the dramaturg, you can edit your script as you go for accuracy of the location, the costumes, and dialect, etc. In this chapter, I will introduce the meaning of the word dramaturg and teach you more about the role of the dramaturg in the theatre. I want to also prepare you for feedback and questions that are destined to come up from your readers and supporters. I want you to be ahead of the game as you work to be influential in your role as a developed playwright.

Time and Location Matters A lot.

Time and location matter tremendously when creating characters and advancing the plot of your play. It's as simple as soda vs. pop. When you get to know your characters, you have to understand the world that they live in. AlthoughI currently reside in Atlanta, I am from South Florida, and we drink sodas, Chek sodas, to be exact, from Winn-Dixie. My favorite soda is the Green Apple Soda. Listen, don't knock it until you try it. I'm not really a soda fan and they probably load them with sugar, so I only drink them when I go home to visit. Where is my traveling crew? I am not ignorant to the fact that Winn-Dixie isn't everywhere in the world. If you haven't been to certain states, you may not know what Winn-Dixie is. And even if you have been to Winn-Dixie in the state that you are in physically, you may have never had the opportunity to taste or acknowledge the Green Apple treat as a soda. Furthermore, if you have that opportunity, you might probably call it pop, depending on where you're from.

Playwrights have to understand that as time changes, so do locations. When using a map, you know that landmarks and buildings change just as fast as they can throw them up. How many times have you gone back to a place you know like the back of your hand only to find out that it has been repainted, demolished, or totally remodeled? Knowing about the location and time keeps the play interesting, engaging and relevant. Small details can help create the setting and add culture and a sense of place to the character.

Ensure they Have the Skills to Survive.

You want characters to be able to communicate with the other characters. Just like in life, language barriers can present a problem. Oftentimes people struggle to connect if they have a problem communicating. Failure to get your characters to speak the language used in the location that they're in is an additional obstacle. Make sure you allow them to speak the dialect, wear appropriate costumes, and use appropriate body language. Think of your characters like they are affiliated with a gang. I would hate for them to be on the wrong side, with the wrong attire, using the wrong body language.

Be Ready for Inquiry.

Theatre thrives off of constructive criticism, and so will your play. Plain and simple, do your research so that your play is authentic and so the audience won't be left with a lot of questions. As a good playwright, you will makesure that the questions are answered throughout the play. I have years of experience in predicting questions as a teacher. Teachers are notorious for predicting the questions that their students will have. Like teachers, playwrights have to be ready for inquiry. Have you ever written a play based in Africa and incorporated sweet potato pie only to find out they didn't know what that was? Just me, I get it, lessons learned, but be ready for questioning. I changed that sweet potato pic to another succulent dessert and incorporated the feedback into the draft. Even after the show, you will still get questions that will totally throw you off. It's okay to incorporate it into your final script and keep it moving. As a self-publisher, you can update your script whenever you choose to.

Look Up Name Meanings.

I love my name. I had the pleasure of being named at the Miami International Airport by Minister Louis Farrakhan. One of my biggest joys, besides having a public figure name me, is the fact that my name has meaning. How did I know that my name has significant meaning? I looked it up. You should do the same for the characters inside of

Be the Dramaturg

your play. Be a good dramaturg and research the names before you put them inside of a script. Take time picking names that go with the character's personality and will motivate you to continue their story.

It is also taboo in the theater to give your characters' names that start with the same first initial, like Sarah and Sally. When technicians work hard to notate blocking and cues in the script, it becomes a hassle with the characters having the same first initials. If you give your character similar names, the notation will look like: SAR (Sarah) and SAL (SALLY) enter SL (stage left). Take my word for it; it causes problems for the stage crew. Though it only takes a little more effort, it's time that the professional can put it elsewhere. Also, don't do too much by creating character names that the actors struggle with saying. Time is money.

Notes

Notes

CHAPTER 6

Find Your Target Audience

"And that's what people want to see when they go to the theater. I believe at the end of the day; they want to see themselves – parts of their lives they can recognize. And I feel if I can achieve that, it's pretty spectacular. "
-*Viola Davis*

Again representation matters in theater, and I hope that every person in the world will find a play that they can relate to. It would make me sleep better at night knowing that every audience member in the world will have a character that they can identify with. If you have ever had a play or a character that spoke to you, do not take it for granted. We all have issues, and I hope that your next play will reach someone else and change their life for the better. To do that, you are going to have to find your target audience member. Who is this play for? What is the message that you would deliver to them? How can they use it to change their world? Silencing your voice as a playwright can be detrimental to the person that needs to hear it.

Identify Your Audience

We Identify our audience based on three core categories:

a. **Demography**: age, sex, education, income, cultural background, etc.
b. **Interest:** What are they looking for? What do they like to read and watch?

c. **Purchase Intentions:** What kind of productions do they like to go to? What kind of plays do they like to watch?

It's important to look at all three categories when identifying your audience.

You can test this theory with this story. My school's chorus went to see an opera. The students begged me to go. I said, "Opera, I believe I made it clear that operas are not my interest". My students know I'm a script person and appreciate it when it has little music. I love music, but I love dialogue. I can enjoy a good musical but sometimes I rather stop singing and say what they mean.

I mostly attend shows that are of interest to me. Though I have mad respect for theatre history, I tend to gear toward the '60s and thereafter. Just like the people that fill my audience, I like plays highlighting issues affecting my cultural background. To continue my story, the students went to see their "little opera" and lo and behold it was *Porgy and Bess*! I was so disappointed in myself. The students knew my purchase intentions, they were familiar with my demographics, yet they neglected the fact that *Porgy and Bess* was of interest to me. Black Arts are significant to theatre history. Why didn't they tell me the opera was *PORGY AND BESS*! After attending the show and finding out what Porgy and Bess was about they should have known it was right up my alley. My interest in the story would outweigh the fact that it was an opera.

Lesson Learned: Consider your audience, pay attention to shifts in interest and events. Use your authentic voice. In doing so you may find an audience you haven't considered before.

Find the Beauty in YOUR Play.

No play is the same. Westside Story is loosely based on Romeo and Juliet however the characters, setting, dialogue is different. Both of them are beautiful productions.

I believe that beautiful plays challenge your thinking, make you feel some type of way inside, make you look at things from different perspectives, and inspire you somehow. Your future play may be an adaptation of a classic and that in no way takes away from its beauty.

Good ideas and great plays make you think. I hope this book is doing the same for you. I hope you are ready for the challenge. I'd love to know that you are following along, highlighting, sharing your thoughts with a friend, and being inspired to use my tactics in the play you are writing. Share your three favorite tips from this book at: bonus.bookedplaywright.com.

Be Creative and Take Risks.

Most of us look at our family and friends as our biggest support system. That doesn't mean they are a part of your target audience, however. Your target audience lives in a world where they have an issue keeping them awake at night and waiting for you to help them navigate it. They want to see something in your play with which they can connect emotionally and find clarity.

People will read/watch your work the first time simply because it's you or because they know your "mama nem" After the first time, sometimes they won't be inclined to return and make the next purchase of your play or ticket again, and here is why: They are not in your TARGET Audience. YOU were simply their TARGET . . . that is all. It's all personal, baby. Some people purchase tickets just to see what you are doing. They spectate to see if they can and will do the same, write a script and produce it. Or they wait around as you work diligently just to see what your obstacles entail when it comes to publishing and marketing your play. It's a valuable lesson. You continue to be creative, put out good content, and your audience will find you.

Brand Your Play.

This is for my self-publishing authors who hope to produce their play and later upload their play to Amazon, Ingram Sparks, or another self-publishing platform. Don't get too caught up in all the details, but your brand matters. It's the first thing people see about your work. I want people to know your work, from the audition flyer to the cover of your play script. People should be able to look at the cover of your play and find out a little bit about you as the creative being you are. You can go with the fancy cardstock cover with the Title, Subtitle, and Byline and put your contact info later in the script.

If you are going to put artwork on the front of your manuscript, hire a professional graphic designer to create it. Invest in someone that knows how to use design software to make you a nice

Find Your Target Audience

audition notice and flyer. I often hear playwrights discuss having their child or family member draw the cover because it's significant to them, but the significance may not be the same for your reader. I would much rather you use a picture from your first production than use botched-up art. If you are going to market to a specific reader or a specific type of audience member, be sure that your cover reflects it. It is the goal that many producers will get inspiration from the cover to add to their production flyer of your work.

Notes

Find Your Target Audience

Notes

Notes

CHAPTER 7

Be the Architect of Your Play

"Keep Your Hands Moving. Writing is rewriting."
-August Wilson

Be the Architect of Your Play

An architect builds, but they also plan, design, and oversee their work. As a playwright, you want to oversee your work pre-production, during production, and post-production. You should always make plans for changes and rewriting. Rewriting is challenging, but it's a necessary step in the playwriting process. In my program, I teach my clients to rewrite throughout like an architect. Every time they get to a pivotal step in their script, or when I make suggestions, they are tasked with going back and redesigning it. It's important to shift your mindset to acknowledge that redo's and repeats are a gift from the galaxy. It doesn't stunt your growth; it enhances it. It's not a setback; it's a setup for something greater. Like the songwriter says, "Greater is coming." I am going to lead you through an interactive workshopping experience, one that you'll actually enjoy.

We want your play to be all you plus any questions a dramaturg would have. You may think all of this a daunting and sometimes tedious task, but we'll get through it together. It's so important that we take advantage of the beauty of workshopping.

Work It First

To be the best, you have to work at it. Think about this: Every person has a job in theatre. If the audience doesn't do its job by demonstrating theatre etiquette and clapping appropriately, it taints the entire experience. Playwrights put the work in ahead of time when nobody's watching and stick around at the end when everybody's watching. That's a big deal.

W-Wait, have an authorized person listen to you and read your work. Many people catch their mistakes by reading aloud.

O-ONLY listen. After you read your work aloud, it's important that you do not describe, respond, or explain.

R-Real Listen. We cannot say it enough. Do not say a mumbling word.

K-Know that you WILL get a response. You may not like it. You may somewhat disagree with it, but know that it will be constructive and never destructive. We want to see you win.

I-Input what worked and ask questions for guidance and direction.

T- "Thank you for the feedback" is always a good response. Ultimately, you are the playwright, and you will make the final decision, so why not listen and incorporate constructive feedback?

When you have people's destiny tied to your script, you must commit to putting the time in. Working will set you up for valuable feedback.

Bring It All Together.

"Everything works out in the end. If it hasn't worked out yet, then it's not the end."
-Tracy McMillan

Your character lives a whole life within the show's run time. Ensuring that their lives come together is a way of showing gratitude to the story. You would not want anyone to leave you high and dry. Go back and read the inciting incident. Have all of the obstacles been resolved? How did the falling action provide clarity? Was it resolved? If you can't determine the resolution of the hindrance, consider putting it in the next play. Make it a duology or, if you are like Sophocles, a trilogy.

Hire an Editor.

Two eyes are better than one, and more eyes will do the trick. Be sure to cross out, input additional details, and edit misspellings and mishaps. Finally, don't forget to italicize, capitalize, criticize; just do NOT plagiarize. Once you have looked over your work, dig a little deeper and have an editor look for mistakes. You've worked so hard to complete your script, so hire a professional to ensure that your grammar is correct. It's a bonus to hire an editor that is also familiar with formatting. Don't be afraid of the red pen. You are not alone, and hiring an editor will, as a result, lessen your level of frustration as you draw closer to completinga script.

Visit bonus.bookedplaywright.com for additional software I recommend for formatting your play.

Plan Your Reading

The playwright isn't finished after the ink dries on the script. After you create your play script, you should schedule a reading. Do it within a few weeks of finishing your draft. Look at today's date on the calendar and plan your reading one month from this date. Reading is fun, and you learn a lot about the tone of the play.

You can solicit actors to serve as cast members. The actors can help you with dialogue and stage directions. You should continue to work on your play beyond opening night to ensure that it's ready to be published. The good news is that you can still edit your script again after curtain. Add lines that stood out to you after you've heard the actors' improvisation, stage directions, and action. Play production is a process, and I highly suggest you embrace it as a self-published playwright. Readings are like presales to a book; it gives people a sneak peek, gets them to talk about your play, and initiates discussions. That's publicity in a sense, and I expect nothing but your very best.

Notes

Notes

Conclusion

I'd like to believe that I'm the best playwriting coach in the world because I believe in you. I know that every single person walking this earth has a story to tell. I have the gift of helping you turn your story into a play. The young girl in me decided one day to change a holiday play at church into something more modern that would grab the teens in the audience. I succeeded and ended up packing the house. I know that you can do the same, create a plan to tackle issues in our society, grow beyond barriers set for self-published writers, and finish your play script. I promise you that you can do it if you write on a theme that you are passionate about. Don't give up; somebody out there wants and needs to hear what you have to say.

Congratulations again on making a conscious decision to read this book and implement the steps I've described. I know that you will strive and drive in the enlightening and entertainment field. Don't put this book down and forget your

Conclusion

commitment to turning your story into a play and empowering your community.

Before you embark on your playwright journey, let me tell you what your very next step should be: Get your play script draft written in the next 2-4 weeks, visit bonus.bookedplaywright.com to get tips and tools to help you along the way, and contact me so I can help you quickly implement the strategies to write your culturally relevant play and get it in front of your target audience.

Curtain Call

Hire Khalia to Speak at your Event
www.bookedplaywright.com/speakup

Presentation Topics:

Create Your Own Stage: Don't wait for others to share your story.

As a self-published playwright, you will have to market your play until you can build your team. Marketing your play allows you to ignite passion in your readers and viewers while allowing you to hone and embrace your story. No one can steal your story because it's tied to a purpose given solely to you. As a playwright, you will establish connections with your audience that only you can access and fulfill.

Participants will learn:
1. How to reach your audience members even when they are not expecting you?
2. The Three-Step K(P)2 Method to get you started with your play.

3. How to authentically share your story so your audience will relate and trust you on their journey to embracing your message.

How to Produce a Culturally Relevant Play in 12 Weeks or Less?

To give your audience access to a communal learning experience, you should use the arts. The arts serve as a mechanism of social change, and you should use them to provide culturally appropriate shows for your community.

Participants will learn:

1. The Three-Step K(P)2 Method to help you deliver quality content to your audience.
2. How to Pitch your work to community liaisons to obtain support and grants?
3. How to be a team player as a member of the production team to balance the task of producing original work?
4. How to budget your play production to ensure contractors and venues are paid in a timely manner?

Red Carpet

Wess Walters Associates
Website: workwithwess.com
FB: Wess Walters and Associates
Instagram: Wess Walters

Courageous Counseling & Consulting
FB: couregeouscounseling
Instagram: @CouregeousCounseling

New Phoenix Solutions Educational LLC
FB: newphoenixsolutions
Instagram: @newphoenixsolutions

We SLAY Body Contouring & Beauty Boutique
Instagram:@weslay_beautyboutique

The Morse Actors Studio
FB: Broadusrestorations
Instagram:@BroadusRestorations

Divine Rootz
FB: divinerootz954
Instagram: @lisha_layedit

Preferred 1st Cleaning Solutions D.B.A. Building Stars
FB: rickey.culbreath.92

Sadior LLC
FB: mrmarc5
Instagram: @MrMarc5

T.C.M Educational Solutions

Realtor Kashima
Website: kpeters.youratlantahomesearch.com
FB: RealtorKashima
Instagram: @realtorkashima

A Book & A Dream
FB: dejamonet
Instagram: @authorpamelahayes

Grace and Mercy International Ministries Helping Hands

Ascension Business Solutions

Red Carpet

Black Girls in Cyber
FB: Blackgirlsincyber
Instagram: @talyaparker.co

Hands of Worth Cleaning, LLC

Mwanga Wa Oshun Program

Latonya's Peace of Cake

Teach Pray Love Brand
FB: Teach Pray Love Brand
Instagram:
@teachpraylovebrand

Made in the USA
Monee, IL
29 January 2022